For   *Eero Felix Long*

Sing salutations with the songbirds, the day has just begun.

Send a *wave* to the *ocean*,

Drift among the clouds,

dive
as
deep
as
the
sea.

feel

majestic

as a

mountain!

Feel *misty* with a *waterfall,* teary-eyed with the dew.

Babble with a cheerful *brook,* ripen with the *fruit.*

Run *rapid* with a *river,* roll *gently* with the *hills.*

Squelch along in *squishy* mud, *revel* in the *thrills!*

Whisper to the trees, listen for hushed applause.

Be
 lazy
   as
  an
afternoon,
            peaceful
               as   a
             pause.

Glory like a sunset,

Laugh along with *thunder*,

light up a *stormy* sky.

Give the moon a tickle, shoot among the stars.

Sigh goodnight to the heavens, blow a kiss to a friend.

PNW Locations of

Give the Moon a Tickle:

(In order of appearance)

Hug Point State Park, Arch Point, *Oregon Coast*
Western Meadowlark, State Bird of Oregon, Rogue Valley, *Oregon*
Twin Rocks in the Pacific Ocean, Rockaway Beach, *Oregon Coast*
Clouds over Lincoln City, *Oregon Coast*
Orca Whales, Strait of Juan de Fuca, *Washington State / Canada border*
Painted Hills, Wheeler County, *Eastern Oregon*
Heceta Head Lighthouse State Scenic Viewpoint, *Oregon Coast*
Wooden Shoe Tulip Farm and Vineyard, Woodburn, *Oregon*
Salmon Street Springs, Willamette River Waterfront, Portland, *Oregon*
Cape Meares, Tillamook County, *Oregon Coast*
Mt. Hood, *Oregon*
Bee in Foxglove, Astoria, *Oregon*
Butterfly in Lavender, Gladstone, *Oregon*
Multnomah Falls, Historic Columbia River Highway, *Oregon*
Cherries growing in The Dalles, *Oregon*
Farms and Ranches in Dufur, *Oregon*
Kite surfers in Hood River, *Oregon*

Great Blue Heron at Nehalem Bay, Garibaldi, *Oregon Coast*

Wind River, Carson, *Washington State*

Deer in Snow, Chenowith, The Dalles, *Oregon*

Gracie snoozing by the Campfire, Secret Spot, *Oregon*

The Wreck of the Peter Iredale, Warrenton, *Oregon*

Wheat Farm, Wasco County, *Eastern Oregon*

Haystack Rock, Cannon Beach, *Oregon*

Crater Lake, Klamath County, *Oregon*

The Moon in the *night sky*

The Pleiades Constellation, and Milky Way
over the Three Sisters, *Cascade Mountain Range*

Vista House, Crown Point, Scenic Columbia River Gorge, *Oregon*

Cathedral Park under St. John's Bridge, Portland, *Oregon*

Thunder Island, Cascade Locks, Scenic Columbia River Gorge,
Oregon / Washington State Border

A special thank you to Sarah *Chambers*, Tommy *Conway*, Amanda *Remington Hoey*, Willie *Riese*, Robert *Sumner, and* Sarah *Weber* for sharing your inspiring photos !

This book is dedicated to :

Bob and Norma Davidson,   *Hal and Edla Allen,*
Felix and LaDonna Durand,   *Bruce and Jan Allen,*
and Steve and Paula Long:

our *grandparents and parents* who *instilled a love*

for our *home terrain*

in the *Pacific NW,*

and a *spirit of adventure* to always *keep exploring.*

Printed by Libri Plureos GmbH in Hamburg, Germany